EXPLORING WORLD CULTURES

China

Ruth Bjorklund

Cavendish
Square

New York

Published in 2016 by Cavendish Square Publishing, LLC
243 5th Avenue, Suite 136, New York, NY 10016

Library of Congress Cataloging-in-Publication Data

Bjorklund, Ruth.
China / Ruth Bjorklund.
pages cm. — (Exploring world cultures)
Includes bibliographical references and index.
ISBN 978-1-50260-592-4 (hardcover) ISBN 978-1-50260-591-7 (paperback) ISBN 978-1-50260-593-1 (ebook)
1. China—Juvenile literature. I. Title.

DS706.B55 2016
951—dc23

2015006657

Editorial Director: David McNamara
Editor: Kristen Susienka
Copy Editor: Cynthia Roby
Art Director: Jeffrey Talbot
Designer: Joseph Macri
Senior Production Manager: Jennifer Ryder-Talbot
Production Editor: Renni Johnson
Photo Research: J8 Media

Printed in the United States of America

Contents

Introduction

China is an old civilization. It started thousands of years ago. The first Chinese people were very smart. They knew how to farm, and how to make pottery and tools. They studied the stars, could read and write, and traded items with other countries. They also had a leader called an emperor who ruled them.

Today the people of China are very close to their families. They believe in honesty, respect, and working hard. They enjoy art and music. Throughout the year, they celebrate exciting festivals.

China is a big country. It has deserts, rivers, grasslands, farms, and tall mountains. Many animals live in the forests and mountains. China is still growing, and it is one of the most powerful nations in the world. It is a special place with lots of history. China is an exciting country to see and visit.

A Chinese boy holds up his country's flag.

This map of China shows the main cities and rivers.

China is the largest country in Asia. It borders three seas and fourteen countries. China has three main areas: eastern, southern, and northwestern.

There are many rivers in the eastern area. The major rivers are the Yellow and the Yangtze. Many farms line the river valleys. The northwestern area has mountains and deserts. Rare animals such as yaks, camels, and snow leopards live there. The southern area has mountains, canyons, and **highlands**. Mount Everest, the tallest mountain on Earth, is in the Himalayan Mountains.

The Baiji

A rare freshwater dolphin called the Baiji lives only in the Yangtze River.

The climate in China is different in each area. In the east and northwest, summers are hot and winters are cold. Southern China has better temperatures but is often rainy.

FACT!

Bamboo is a tree native to Chinese. It can grow 90 feet (27 meters) in just five weeks.

People have lived in China for centuries. The ancient Chinese were great inventors. They invented papermaking, printing, and the compass.

This old painting on silk shows an emperor greeting visitors.

For centuries, families called **dynasties** ruled China. The leaders, called emperors, sent their armies to destroy enemies and take over land. Then in 1912, Chinese rebels defeated the last dynasty. Their leader, Dr. Sun Yat-Sen, was the first president of China.

Madame Soong Ching-Ling and Dr. Sun Yat-Sen

In 1945, a man named Mao Zedong took control of China. He believed the government should own all factories and farms and that people should share wealth. He took land from the rich and tore down ancient buildings.

Later, other leaders made changes. Today, China is a fast-growing and powerful nation.

FACT!

Chinese emperors built the Great Wall of China to defend against enemies. It is 5,500 miles (8,850 kilometers) long.

Government

China's government is unique. There is one major political party, the Communist Party of China. A **constitution** was signed in 1982. This document created three **branches** of government: executive, legislative, and judicial.

The Chinese flag. The large yellow star represents the Communist Par

The Capital

More than 21 million people live in the busy capital city of Beijing.

The State Council forms the executive branch. The council includes a leader called a premier, vice premiers, and ministers. There is also a president. He or she and the leaders of the Communist Party choose the premier. The premier runs the government and the president is the head of state.

The State Council and the president are elected by members of the legislative branch. Their job is to make laws. The judicial branch is made up of the Supreme People's Court and local people's courts.

FACT!

The Chinese army is an important part of the government. It is called the People's Liberation Army.

China has a big **economy**. More than 700 million people are farmers. Most farmers live in the valleys by the Yellow and Yangtze rivers. They grow wheat and rice. Rice is the

Three farmers tend their rice crops on a hillside.

country's most important crop. These crops are sold around the world.

FACT!

Shanghai is one of the world's richest cities.

China sells more items to other countries than any other country. Skilled factory workers make computers, TVs, cell phones, clothing, shoes, furniture, and cars. They send their products overseas.

China also has many natural resources,

The Three Gorges Dam crosses the Yangtze River.

such as lumber, coal, and oil. China gets most of its energy from coal. Waterpower is also important. China has the world's largest dam. The dam uses waterpower to make electricity.

The Silk Road

Ancient Chinese people traded with other nations. The Silk Road was a 4,000-mile (6437 km) route across ancient China. People used this road to trade with other countries.

The Environment

China has big cities filled with lots of people. People working in cities and in factories use a lot of energy. They have cars, trucks, buses, and buildings that burn fuel and coal. Because of this, many Chinese cities are polluted. Rivers and lakes are also dirty. Many animals suffer, too.

Many people in Beijing wear masks to protect themselves from dirty city air.

Bad Air

In January 2013, Beijing experienced very bad **smog**. The air was so dirty that people wore masks and could not see well.

One-quarter of animals listed as extremely endangered live in China.

Animals need wild places in which to live and grow. Loggers cut down forests. People build on the land. This means many animals are in danger of disappearing forever.

A giant panda in one of China's bamboo forests

China is trying to make the environment safer. They pass laws to clean the air and water, and to protect the animals. More people use energy made by water, wind, and the sun.

Women dressed in clothing from the ancient Han dynasty

There are 1.3 billion people living in China. It is the most populated country in the world. Many Chinese people live in the country, but more people are moving to work in cities. Today Chinese families are small. Laws limit most parents to one child.

Tibet

Tibet was an independent country, but China took over in 1959. Many Tibetans moved away, including most of the people's leaders.

Nearly all native Chinese people belong to the Han **ethnic** group. In ancient China, the Han dynasty brought many groups together to make one. But this is not the only ethnic group. There are fifty-five other ethnic groups, including Mongols, Tibetans, and Uighurs. Mongols live near Mongolia. Tibetans live in the Himalayan Mountains. The Uighurs are related to Turkish people. They live in western China.

FACT!

Han Chinese people make up 20 percent of the population of the whole world.

Life for Chinese people differs depending on where they live. People who live in cities have small families. Husbands and wives have jobs. Many children go to school seven days

Chinese families like to live, work, and play together.

a week. People living in the country may have larger families who work together. Children have chores, and not all men and women work outside the home. Many families have other relatives living with them, too.

Visitors

Visitors are always welcome. They usually bring small gifts.

Transportation and housing are also different. People in the city often live in small, expensive apartments. They might drive a car. People in the country live in groups of houses that face a central

Chinese children help with this family's wheat harvest.

courtyard. Few people own a car or truck. Most use bicycles, horses, oxen, or donkey carts to travel.

FACT!

Many groups of people who live in the mountains are **nomads.** They live in round tents called yurts.

This Tibetan temple overlooks a village high in the
Himalayan Mountains.

In China, religion was not allowed for many years.
Today, however, many religions are practiced
in China. Some of these religions are very old.
China's more popular religions are Confucianism,
Taoism, and Buddhism. Confucianism teaches
values of family, respect, and hard work. Taoism
teaches that people should be healthy, kind, and in

Yin and Yang

The Tao yin/yang symbol shows opposites living in harmony.

harmony with nature. Buddhism came from India. Its founder, Buddha, was a prince who taught people to be honest, useful, peaceful, and to care for the environment.

There are other religions in China, too. Islam and Christianity are also practiced. Many centuries ago, Islam was brought to China by **Muslim** traders who traveled the Silk Road. Christians first came to China in the thirteenth century. Today Christianity is one of the largest religions practiced in China.

Officially, China is an **atheist** country. However, today more people follow a religion.

Language 语

Several languages are spoken in China. The most common language is Mandarin. It is spoken by 70 percent of the people. Today many people doing business with China also are learning Mandarin. Mandarin is

It takes much practice to learn to write Chinese characters.

the language taught in China's schools, but many schools also teach their students' home language. Lots of people also learn English.

Most ethnic groups have their own language. The Mongols speak Mongolian, and several ethnic groups speak different forms of Tibetan. The Uighurs and other groups living in western China speak a Turkish language.

Calligraphy

Beautiful handwriting, called calligraphy, is very important to the Chinese people.

The Chinese people do not write using letters. Instead, they use characters, or drawings, that describe ideas, actions, and things. There are more than fifty thousand characters.

FACT!

Most people in the world cannot read Chinese writing. Pinyin is a system that translates Chinese sounds into words non-Chinese readers can understand.

The Chinese people enjoy different art forms. They are skilled in artwork, crafts, sewing, and theater. They are known for their paintings, pottery, and silk. In ancient China, potters used a special type of white clay

Dancers perform the dragon dance in a Lunar New Year's parade.

to make pottery. Today China continues to make excellent items. Skilled carvers make statues from ivory and jade. Weavers make silk cloth.

FACT!

The Chinese invented fireworks around two thousand years ago.

The Color Red

In China, the color red means joy and good luck. On New Year's Day, children are given red envelopes stuffed with money.

Music, dance, and telling stories are important pastimes. Chinese musicians play different string instruments. Many people attend operas

People participate in an exciting Dragon Boat race.

and plays. People also enjoy poetry.

Every year, Chinese festivals are filled with songs, dances, costumes, and fireworks. Major events include Chinese Lunar New Year and the Dragon Boat Festival.

The official name for Ping-Pong is table tennis.

Chinese people are hardworking. When they have time to enjoy themselves, they have many fun choices. In cities, people go to movies, operas, concerts, and restaurants. Everyone enjoys games such as cards, chess, and mah-jongg, which is a game played with colorful tiles. Kite making and kite flying are traditional pastimes.

Martial Arts

Many people practice wushu, which is the Chinese word for martial arts.

Chinese people believe in staying healthy. People of all ages practice an exercise called Tai Chi. Children begin their school day with exercises such as jumping jacks and pushups.

Chinese schools and factories set aside special places for their students or workers to play sports. Popular sports are gymnastics, basketball, badminton, swimming, Ping-Pong, and tennis.

FACT!

In the 1970s, Ping-Pong became a very important sport for China. It helped them start relationships with other countries around the world.

Mealtimes are special in China. Families and friends eat together. Food is served on large plates and everyone shares. People use chopsticks to eat their food.

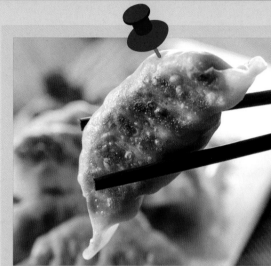

Fried dumplings are delicious when dipped in sauces.

Chinese people cook with fresh ingredients. Favorite vegetables include corn, eggplant, onions, garlic, and ginger. People also eat chicken, duck, pork, beef, and lamb. Rice is the main food eaten at meals. However, many cooks also prepare noodles to go with their meat and vegetables. Cooks in central China are known for making spicy foods with hot red peppers.

Tea
People drink tea all day long. There are three types: green, red, and black.

Sweet and sour pork, fried noodles with vegetables, and spring rolls are popular dishes. Dumplings filled with chopped meat and vegetables are a favorite dish on New Year's Day.

FACT!

Chinese people cook food quickly. Cooks use a hot, round pan called a wok to cook the food.

Glossary

atheist   A person who does not believe in God or a religion.

branch   A part of the government.

constitution   A document that describes a country's laws.

dynasties   Families or groups that rule for several generations.

economy   The wealth and natural resources of a country.

ethnic   A word describing groups of people who have the same customs, religion, and race.

highlands   Hilly areas of land.

Muslim   A person who follows the religion of Islam.

nomads   People who move from place to place.

smog   A thick smoke that comes from pollution.

Find Out More

Books

Mattern, Joanne. *We Visit China*. Your Land and My Land: Asia. Hockessin, DE: Mitchell Lane Publishers, 2014.

Shea, Therese. *Foods of China*. Culture in the Kitchen. New York: Gareth Stevens Publishing, 2011.

Websites

Ancient China for Kids

china.mrdonn.org

TIME for Kids: China

www.timeforkids.com/destination/china

Video

Chinese New Year Lion Dance in Hong Kong

www.youtube.com/watch?v=J7vVUQmR8Vo

Watch the traditional Chinese Lion Dance performed on the Chinese Lunar New Year.

Index

About the Author

Ruth Bjorklund lives on an island near Seattle, Washington, with her family. She has written many books for young people. She and her son visited China and hiked along the Great Wall and in the Himalayan Mountains. China is amazing!